Desire by me
adam Shove

Desire
Copyright © 2022 adam Shove
DARK THIRTY POETRY PUBLISHING
ISBN: 978-1-7397975-2-2
All Rights Reserved

Shove, adam
First edition

Artwork by
Valeria Auväärt

DTPP6

All rights are reserved. No part of this publication may be reproduced, stored in a retrieval system or transmitted in any form or by any means, electronic, mechanical, photocopying, recording or otherwise, without prior permission from the author. Unless it's a tattoo, that's fine.

Books by adam Shove

Eriatarka 2007
I Just Destroyed My Heart In 764 Seconds 2008
In The East March, White Roses In Black Paper 2009
Convalesce Convene 2010
Nineteen 2010
Punk Poet Prophet 2011
I Feel So Bad, I Thought You'd Want To Know 2011
Each Realisation I'm New 2012
My Heart Is A Mausoleum 2013
The Atmosfear Of The Blank Door 2013
Lucid 2015
Laconic 2016
Postcards To Dogmatic Voices 2017
...and The Past Was Now 2017
Last Night And This Morning 2018
The Vodka Diaries 2019
Coast 2020
Photogenic Afterthoughts 2020
Fling 2021
Desire 2022

DARK THIRTY POETRY PUBLISHING

For Valeria, you were perfect.

Taksopark

You told me winter was your season,
I admired your beauty
Even though it's Sagittarius
Not Libra region.
Nothing ever lasts,
We both knew that
When the snow starts to thaw.
White roses salivate on your skin,
This was how I navigate
The contours you dictate.
It hadn't even been a night,
While we started to calibrate.
I didn't know your mistakes,
I was distracted
You had seduced me
Between the notes of James Blake.

Pirita

How many more times do I need to declare,
I sat at the underpasses here in Tallinn
Writing so many letters
While running fingers through your hair.
I started to see the insides of your eyes
Magnetise with Aurora,
All the while I could concise
That you're perfect nitrogen flora.
Now all I have is your tattoos
Embedded within my brain,
Flowers resting on a reservoir.
Sea glass lavender at the day breaks,
The world through the wormhole
Has us kissing
While both holding the handlebars.
Poetic thoughts when waking up to the snow
Of this eternal winter.

Tehnika

The old town begins to remind me
Of a snow globe I bought my niece,
The citadel and cathedral walks
Leave waffle prints
From where I've been.
The neighbours have moved,
Guess there was an issue with the lease.
I adore how you look
When you wear my sweatshirt,
Can I say how I find desires in your figure,
Using my tees as a keyword.
You always wear blue
For the few hours the sun is out,
I rather see you in white.
When you don't it puts my heart into doubt,
The way your skin glows in candlelight.
A new one lit for every poem I have for you,
And if the house burns down
It shows how you are
Who I can't live without.

Meeliku

Do you remember
When I first saw you in Amsterdam,
You told me your name
And I was too swooned
To think of an anagram.
Now I hope we haunt this house
So the next occupants have to call ghostbusters,
Burning sage
Saying no need to haunt us youngsters.
Was it you or me
That was the first to enquire the desire
For a matching tattoo?
Unfiltered sky,
And the ground is black and yellow.
The sea became calm
As I went back to hibernate,
You my mermaid
My eyes wide shutting view.

Karikakra

She took my name
While I took her nationality,
Eventually it'll all fall apart;
She reminded me nothing lasts forever
It all works in entropy.
Alpha to omega,
for you I'd walk to Tallinn
All the way from Odesa.
A staccato of sound,
mesmerising are you even real?
I don't know what I found,
Questioned so many times
How should I cognise what anyone wants?
I'm so far brazenly cold,
Matching tattoos
And everything else we do hold.

Pronksi

And in those hours
Between when we both fall asleep,
I became crazy in my thoughts
As they're all cheap.
My hive mind flickers
On multiple levels of you,
Dysfunctional thoughts happen,
But I don't complain
Even when early morning is fashion.
Zero dark thirty the clock reads,
This void of soundtrack
Except the outside streets.
The barely legible drunken slurs,
I couldn't pick out a word
For this esoteric verse.
Only you left my pulse hectic,
My eyes clocked into you October seventh,
When it comes to clocking out
I hold no intention.

Liivaku

When I met you
I didn't know how this was going to be
In a day,
Let alone now.
While now I scan the dictionary
Like a pterodactyl
Looking for words to enjoin,
Without saying the words
That I'm required to enounce.
Now I try to be how you described,
What was it beaudoin.
A renaissance now ensconce
Words that make us starve,
An empyrean would be the section of your skin
My words inscribed.
To tell the truth it's all impulsive,
Even when overthought
You were more seductive.
The sound of walking in the snow,
While things here are more than I imbibed.

Kanuti

You were the cosmology I was enthralled by,
We grifted the world
With our prestige champagne kisses
For your thigh.
Time wasn't relevant,
Not when we could live as long as a tree.
Do you remember our first date?
That white dress redefined elegance.
And when we fight it tears me apart
Like a child getting its first set of teeth,
Then when it's past
I know that the taste of white chocolate
Is more sweet.
While those nights I'm not with you,
They leave me feeling
More isolated than birth.

Mõisa

I told you how I tripped
When your hair was black,
Peroxide didn't help me stay on my feet.
Another early morning grabbing sheath,
As the switchblade unpacks.
Spotlight happens,
Even when those lights shine by just
fractions.
Breakfast was pancakes,
Didn't you hear
You couldn't turn this commodity
Into a bundle of cash.
The quality of this philosophy
Or monsters of trash.
Doctors tell caution
At soon to be illegal handshakes.
I didn't think you would call
This a ghillie suit,
When it's not.
Caught in the afternoon reflection,
This was our collection
Breaking glass in a slingshot.

Paesilla

You had lost more money
Than I could ever earn,
Loyalty was all you ever asked,
The only thing I had
Was an ampersand between our names
For a kern.
It was while the black circles spin,
Your dulcet tones haunt me
While the windows frosted.
It could have been a jinn.
Today was better than the first time
I saw your lack of textiles,
Still I know we're going for
A better tomorrow.
Surplus of our minimum percentiles.
Pastries for breakfast
With white snow lost here so clear.
Whereas the rain made my vision blurry,
Jazz music oxygenated the atmosphere,
Asking who is was
I said Miles Davis firstly.

Värava

You always hear the sound of a closing door,
The teradynes act like an onomatopoeia,
There was silence
Expect for the sound of my headphones,
I could be sure of your location
From the pheromones.
Meanwhile your hair smells like petunia.
You told me the lights in the empty bottles
Made the home,
My legs trapped,
As yours keep me in place,
All I see is your lipstick
Reflecting in the chrome.
Pulling me in grabbing more than skin,
Ask me in two minutes
I can give descriptives of your lace.

Sirbi

I wanted to out count an abacus
As to how many days
You'd be the purpose
Of my thoughts service,
I don't want to leave
It to the point of damages.
That could just be trepidation,
Sometimes I think I hallucinate,
Then I remember how it's all just you
With how I palpitate.
I find it adorable
How you look over my shoulder
Trying to read my dictation.
I couldn't tell
If this was our reality or fate,
The fabric of time needed stitching
So it stood less chance to switching
From this place.

Paljandi

I just want to hold you
When I smell the melancholia
Drowning out the incense in the air,
I lick the blade clean,
With sorrow in your eyes
Resembling cannellini beans.
The neighbour has a voice
That sounds like a snare drum,
So do you remember
When we first met?
I told you we'd get out of the ghetto,
Yellow buildings in the slums.
Who would the spotlight be on?
How else do you warm
The frostbite of this December?

Tõnismägi

Would I call it an accident?
I swear I didn't mean to add harissa,
I knew this would last
When going vegetarian
Was what you suggested.
Risotto rice laced with a hint of Morocco,
Life was good today
But Monday
Doesn't always show the world in macro.
I asked you not to take all the wine,
Handing me a new bottle
I saw the glistening in your smirk.
I don't remember the jazz playing,
It was original not a rework,
As I dropped the heat
Before adding the last of the stock,
You stepped in closer
Meaning I didn't get to see all of you
Dressed to the nines.

Priisle

People started to listen to me,
I guess I should now have something
To dictate on the stage.
There were movements to what I wanted to say,
And even though the words
Were always the same.
The emphasis was in the emotional depth.
The walls were painted clotted white,
Polka dotted words
That fell into the background
Of what was to be kept.
There are days when I think back
To before these walls,
When I was just waiting on
The distance between us
To be reduced
For the words
I smile at when I introduce.

Urva

Some days I use your shampoo
Just so I have you in the air
When I'm at work,
Blackened macadamia nuts
As my mind is clear.
I followed you
From those grey forgotten streets,
We left that rancid food,
Guess that's why we moved here.
I couldn't get you to be vegetarian,
Recollections of eating Caribbean
Jerk chicken.
Possessions that a year ago
I didn't appreciate,
Now you tell me in bed
To just use the twenty-second letter.
V you want me to abbreviate.

Marja

I didn't want to be selfish
Not sharing you with the parking lot,
This dank winter night acts
Like the inside
Of a cardboard box.
You take my beanie
So I can't run my fingers
Through your locks,
Holy water as a puddle
Freezing over.
Taking the keys from your hand,
Reminding you that I'm the one who is sober.
The fob flickered between my fingers,
Did I tell you
How much I want to trade this in
For a European four seater?
I found it to be ostentatious,
But I kept it for you.
You liked the low ride
How it didn't leave us nameless.

Kivisilla

We started to open up after a few dates,
I had never met a woman
That I'd refer to
As a kintsugi plate.
Enrapturing me in,
As if I were one of the many photographs
That I take of you.
When I noticed the comb in the bathroom,
I guess it all changed then,
Traces of every colour you dyed your hair
Within the bathroom sink.
I often find myself
Lost in the poetry of your skin,
Drowning in the dialect
That we created as a vanryn.
So are we a cognitive architect?
Or am I overthinking
This in retrospect?

Vambola

It's not always a blur,
Sometimes we both prioritise our jobs
Ahead of us;
Most certainly doesn't mean
That when I get home
I'm not wanting
To share a moment like this.
It's been too long
Since I shared a pure thought,
For that I apologise,
My mind wanders often
It makes it hard to reminisce.
Sometimes I'm distracted
By the way you apply your lipstick,
Don't think I'm always one to pluralise.
Macaroons for breakfast,
Shall it be a surprise?
How that perfume you wear
Makes me what's the word,
Infatuated.
I can live until the end of time
And I'll never forget
The passion in your eyes the first night.
I'm sorry I often ramble,
I forgot to tell you
What my pure thought was.

Kaabli

Waking up though it
Was all unknown pleasures,
So long as they were with you
It was more or less what I wanted.
Before I met you I used to draw,
Acrylic paints and charcoal sticks
Only I could manipulate.
Sauerkraut because you asked for it
After the workout,
I ran a lifetime
While the Baltic skyline
Tried to descend into a blackout.
It wasn't even fourteen hundred hours,
The soles of my feet were tense.
I looked at your shoes coloured verdigris,
Copper degrading itself
Before we can all assimilate,
When I wake up in the morning
I don't know the differences.

Endla

I know it's not as often
When I bring home
White wine, roses,
Handmade chocolates and lingerie,
But when I do;
Does it remind you of being 25 again?
I know a decade has past us,
And tomorrow I'm going to surprise you,
White Victoria Secrets.
I didn't need eternity,
Optometry would have failed before then.
It could have been an idea
Within a dream,
White scratched and knuckle blood
John Frusciante Stratocaster,
The night got better
When I saw those teeth
And heard that laughter.

Seli

My mind often casts itself back
To when I first told you that I write,
Your explanation
That I shouldn't write about you.
I should write about life,
This may not be permanent
Like our tattoos.
Entropy is always getting shorter,
But life is a continuous payment of dues.
What the fuck keeps me alive?
Music, you and water.
I ain't perfect,
Never said I was;
I don't have words that echo across
churches,
I couldn't even tell you
If that was incorrect,
I guess it 'twas.
At night Tallinn
Falls as silent as Compton,
The day we walked past the light pollution
And the night sky
Reminded me of sticks of carbon.

Vihuri

If I only had one hundred words
To give you,
There wouldn't be enough,
You're such an imbue status to life.
It's the same feeling
As when we're driving
And I hear the first notes
To TUFF.

Lennusadam

The winter sun is so infrequent,
A year and a half we've been locked inside
Waiting on a change to the season.
At least that's what it feels like,
In the silence
I am able to check our pulse,
Mine is normally 56,
Though when I look into your eyes
It spikes.
I adapted the N on my compass
To show me how to get back to you,
All the while I felt it all
Hit me bulbous.
Spectator,
This was a continuous story
That needed a narrator,
It can't always be from my point of view,
Nails tessellating
As if they were Tetris pieces.
I think I speak for both of us
That we're waiting on warmer weather,
Beaches and time
With both vodka and pizza.

Naaritsa

See this is how I describe you,
The 21st century Mona Lisa,
Tattoo on your leg from afar
Reminds me of a zebra.
Bamboo chair in the bathroom,
I just went off course,
Still life was blue, black and white
Why were they simply lines
And not crossed
Close enough to be Norse.
The vodka dreams I have of you
Are precious but never to be a secret,
More important to me than anything
I should call you El Dorado.
If something is to happen
I hope you let me know,
I'd be on my way to the seppuku,
Life without you
Reminds me of a sword minus the blade;
Seriously an issue.

Pikri

I hope over the next twenty years
We fix into each other
Like a tessellating pattern,
Sorry that's my own babbern,
Sorry I meant to say babble.
Falling back into the way that I cheat,
Not with remembering streets,
More with words in scrabble.
It was both of our desires
To have matching tattoos
We just couldn't decide on what.
Somebody told me never to get a name;
But I'd get yours the day after one of us die,
So we're together when the casket shuts.
Do you recall when you asked me
What I was reading,
The Art Of War,
But it wasn't what I was intending.
The way that you say,
"Come on now, take me to bed.
I'm begging for you
To be removing my threads."
Secretly you know that I'm infatuated
By the way you talk like that.

Haabersti

I'm not content with us both being satisfied,
A habitual shouldn't last for too long.
Maybe what I'm looking for is orbiting us
Too close to be a satellite.
Pillars and chrome fall vacant
Surrounded by hollow metal.
When people ask
What do I nickname you,
Petal.
Because the constant winter
Has hardened us both.
And with three feet of snow,
It's a reminder we're not leaving the house,
We got nowhere to go.
I guess this time
Will let me study your anatomy,
White on white snow outside
And the result of our alchemy.
Just us together,
Can we explore new pleasures?

Sitsi

Do you remember the day that you asked me
To cut my hair short,
Just for you.
The date of that was November fourth.
I cut it again
For when you were going to take me out
For my birthday.
I didn't want to grow it long,
Not for anyone.
Now I'm waiting until I can manipulate my hair
Without the assistance of a hat,
Breakfast consists of swirls
Of toasted cinnamon,
Difficult dialect being strung together;
Professor this is a strain on my ligaments.

Vineeri

And every time you ask me
What was my first time like?
I always give the same answer,
Not as good as when I woke up next to you.
Some mornings I have to shake myself
Like I were a snow globe,
More than words and the teeth marks
On my earlobes.
Petunias fill the room,
Vesuvius footprints from a distant holiday,
Where would you like to go next?
The world shutdown,
Still I want to travel.
We're still here,
And together,
I guess Covid didn't win.

Lauluväljak

And the words that you say leave lipstick marks
On our bedsheets,
Something new for me to save
Beyond the saffron coloured flowers
Enjoying the humidity.
Lines repeated from stranger things,
Sugar spun cookies cooling.
The smell of verivorst
Being cooked our neighbour,
The smell was a metaphor
I was compartmentalising while pouring water.
Behind the roses that you use in the bath,
Are the salts as I unwind
And try to understand the polyrhythms of life,
Long division and math.

Majaka

The world would need a Geiger counter
And still not be able to understand
The chemistry between us,
I can't be sure of the first time
It was definitive,
The way you say my name
With a hint of lust.
It might be repetitive,
All the times I tell you babe
I got your back,
Your sides,
And like that barroom brawl,
Play music at the right tempo,
And I'll be throwing elbows.

Pöörise

I know we don't need to leave the city,
But are there abandoned towns near us?
We have snow on our Baltic shore,
I see how you're dressed
And they all have envy.
Heaven's only five feet tall,
We stand on the outside
Watching our niece and nephew
Run through it.
I wanted D'angelo,
Though they both told us
To play modern music.

Ristiku

The fresh scent of peaches,
The detail in your low ride jeans,
Black and white stripes
A constant reminder
That you're the queen to this scene.
While I want to hear your explanation
As to the rips,
I was going to ask
But I was distracted
By the loose bobbypin grip.
Now everywhere we go it's all visas,
Every photoshoot I go watch you do
I'm breathless,
You really are a weakness.
Do you not step back
And watch as we orbit each other,
I find solace when you say
You'll orbit back to me
Even with the advances of another.

Kalamaja

Acid rain and the lightning storms consume,
I have to make a call on zoom.
You ask me who I'm talking to,
My baby sister,
Goose or Kenz?
Both at the same time,
While I'm discreetly boiling the kettle
To help with a splinter.
Do I need anything from the shop?
You ask
As I hand you the keys to the Benz,
No,
Just a better word for me to rhyme.

Vismeistri

If purgatory
Is spending this lifetime away from you,
I'd rather you got the rapture
So I know that one of us was
Going to have a better tomorrow.
Was this all a philosophical thing?
The eight minutes of sun
This day offered
Is completely insignificant
If I don't get to spend it laying in the snow,
You at my antipode.
A husky walks past
As our eyelashes touch,
You ask me when I use certain words
And I say nonesuch.

Kalmuse Tee

I'm really sorry,
Today I might seem distracted.
I went to see my grandmother
And she didn't recognise my face,
Not even memories stay lasted.
I hope dementia doesn't get to either of us,
Valeria can you please explain to me,
How can you say goodbye to someone
When they say to pass on a message to yourself?
I don't know.

Valdeku

What happened to that corset
You were wearing
At that burlesque photo shoot?
There are lights that illuminate
The moments our advice
Was ignored by my sister.
Jilted events happen,
Tinted intents fashion.
The sugar candy porcelain
Of your skin,
With the kintsugi remnants
And newly delivered tattoos.
If there was something
More important to life,
It hadn't been cut down to size
With a fork and knife,
Words of a necromancer,
Sorcery of the notes
Inside a telecaster.

Oruvärava

I don't enjoy to see those tears
Whether they are joy or sorrow,
It reminds me of an animal
Unable to reach the prey's bone marrow.
Honesty given
When we both have to explain our issues,
Though I overthink monetary values,
That's why my barber is my therapist.
I've never heard you complain,
What was it you called her?
A perfectionist.
Thing is this is real life,
There's no Iron Man
To come and save us all.

Tuisu

What else is there for us to do
At this hour?
You're asleep and I am only still alive
Because my pattern is so broken,
Resembling a jigsaw.
I could have gone running,
I think to myself
What colour will you dye your hair next,
Paprika?
You'd look like a more perfect version
Of Christina Hendricks.
Cinnamon swirls throughout your hair
And what I sent as a text for our breakfast,
The notes that I drifted away to last night
Sound different in the morning.
What else can I say,
Sometimes I get distracted by your sleep
apnoea.

Mustjõe

When I ask you if you can cook dinner
So it's not me late at night,
You know I can teach you.
All the questions that are weak willed
While it could never be considered
Raw heart.
There's something
In how you distract me,
I think you know
Like how you stand in that dress,
Looking as sharp as a citron tart.
Transparent peach,
With black underneath;
You're the queen
In this game of life
Or chess.

Rummukõrtsi

And that time you bit my lip,
Breaking the skin.
It caused me to roll my eyes,
Levitating;
Since when did you
Become a superconductor?
You want me to ask that question,
I'm waiting until Barcelona;
For now say filibuster.
Why didn't I know you in California?
There's so much more than freedom
In our lifetime moments.
I get lost in desires
With the lucid tones
Of your accent.
Sometimes, just sometimes
This spontaneous nature,
Should reach out
To the limits of Canis Major.

Taevakivi

You're this porcelain magnum opus,
In the shop window,
Everybody stops to notice.
Coldest weather
Today is something below zero,
It was always going to happen,
Talons in life
And as I understand
The expiry date to all of this
Shrinks down resembling a Matryoshka doll.
Shall I get another round?
It's not even about the alcohol,
It's about getting your unfiltered
attention.
Are we at the point
When we can read each other's mind?
Let me know.
My eyes constantly admire your waist,
Though you see through the lie
When I say I'm counting snow flakes.

Keskhaigla

And if today you were feeling nostalgic,
Or heavy for a time
That we weren't alive for.
Do you fancy vegan food tonight,
Organic?
I'm cooking,
If you'd rather we can get takeout.
I know when the summer solstice happens
We will do what we always do,
Admire the sun before we head south.
My sister asked are you still able
To do her nails?
Telling me she has a date?
Can you find out what he's like,
I won't get an answer out of her.
I didn't feel like going to the bar,
I wanted to be here for you when you got home.
When you left this morning,
You didn't say goodbye
Or send a selfie.

Gonsiori

I shared a glance
With this platinum blonde,
With gemstones for eyes,
Another day she could have lured me in,
But she wasn't you.
Whenever people ask me to describe you,
All I can ever say is,
Did you ever hear about
The lost Fabergé eggs?
I mean other women can be tasteful,
But you are priceless.
The nights sit still
As the couch is moulded to us
While Black Saint And The Sinner Lady
Spins on the deck.
Parts of that could have been lucid,
How could another woman
Ever take the place of you.

Keemia

I wasn't able to sleep tonight,
It's not the same as normal,
Where the time is integrated
With broken sleep,
I'm sat upright.
All I'm doing
Is looking at your side of the bed,
Waiting on you to push open our door.
I mean this is life,
But are you going to tell me
There's more?
We haven't shared an Instagram post
With our eyes lost in each other in so long,
Those were summer days,
Now I feel the winter wind,
At midnight it's December ten.
And even when the flowers can't grow,
I know that when I wake up
And our eyelashes interlock,
That's when life is beautiful.

Ristaia

Do you remember
When we flew from Miami to New York
Just because
The pizza down south was revolting,
Those are the moments
That I know all this madness
Keeps me floating.
I notice that you shiver less
When you're wearing my coat,
Time goes back,
Still you're what I fill up in my notes.
Landing in Queens
And asking the taxi driver
To take us to Brooklyn for pizza,
Goats cheese, mozzarella and balsamic glaze;
Resembling a zebra.
Boom bap being recorded in the apartment above,
His words all burst to life.
You tell me that Hands Open
Is your favourite song;
Before asking
When am I going to make you my wife.

Kiviku

This was the first trip
I've had away from you in over a year,
I know it was only a few days
But all those months
We were close to each other's throats
During lockdown,
This was needed.
I forgot to take any boxer shorts,
But I packed your shampoo
Just so the smell of macadamia nuts
Is on the pillowcases,
The rain outside
Missing your electromagnetic pulses.
I packed a collection of books,
How much I will read I don't know;
Be nice this week not having to cook.
You sent me a message
Saying that you missed the smell of
samphire,
And then you teased me with the pictures.

Koskla

Since I met you
I don't seem to be able to forget anything,
James Brown drum tracks
Loop in my head.
Samples that I would use
Appear in everything.
Only in your name
Does all this chaos
Start to make sense,
If Picasso were alive
He would have fought me
To muse over you,
He never would have won.
Others would be distracted
By video games and the TV screen.
You know that only for you
Would I wait forever,
What's the expiry date
On this continuous winter?
The weather man says never.
At least it feels like,
I wasn't fully listening.

Randla

I was waiting on the universe
To do something,
While it's all
In the ebbs and flows.
Nothing happens,
Or so it seems,
I'm just one to manipulate time
So it all feels slow.
Imagine an idea,
So powerful it can't be broken.
Even if all this exists
In a Petri dish,
An instant impact has a chance
To fall apart.
Whereas only for you
Would I stand in your way,
Stare death in the eye.
Not blink,
Bare knuckle,
Before I go the full twelve rounds,
Hit me with everything,
If it's for her I'll never go down.

Madala

Last night when I got home,
You were already asleep,
I made sure you were comfortable;
Before I made my way to the couch.
I checked your schedule
Unsure if I needed to make
Any cancellations,
I didn't want to disturb you
Enhancing your frustrations.
You left Netflix on that bad movie
Where the tigers crouch,
I turned it off,
Found my headphones
And drifted away into the ether,
Astral plane,
Is any of this real?
How are you even real?
The lights in you all scream stellar.

Hallivanamehe

Late night ideas
That roll through my head,
Deciding what tomorrow brings,
Mixtape on an actual cassette.
I knew that in the days with you
I didn't need to say I had regrets,
Because time evolves in slow motion,
Salacious wording happens
In the spaces between peace and war.
Last night you said
That your graduation dress
Still looks curvaceous on you,
I met you three weeks later,
I'd want to see you in it;
There's another dress,
Or maybe a few.
These halcyon days
As we sit and watch
The calmness around us.

Telliskivi

If we had met when we were teenagers,
Everyone says
We wouldn't have been students
But truant masters.
Martinis tasted dire
Every time we tried them,
And the olives dried my mouth out
I couldn't even produce phlegm.
P. T. Barnum was prepared to offer
Pretty much anything
For what we have,
I tried to explain
You'll never find this El Dorado
With a fucking Sat Nav.
Quantum ideas
While the spider plant tries its best
To help with the condensation
That we created in the other room.

Kose

The other day
I randomly met your ex,
He tried to warn me about you.
I was left confused,
Telling him,
"Didn't you ever realise
You said her name fully wrong,
Now her hair's no longer blonde,
She's on a different playlist now,
My recommendations;
All these unheard songs."

Räime

How else do I explain
That you occupy spaces
In every aspect of my mind,
I didn't know
What to say next
So long as it had the ability
To rhyme.
How our hair colour is the same,
Can we watch the snow lay outside
From the futon.
An avocado, lettuce and Emmental sandwich,
A base of Grey Poupon.
As simple as it sounds,
That's all I need;
There's already you.
All of this life,
And I spend my evenings
Looking at the sun
Thinking thank god
That it's been you and me.

Hobujaama

This world is full of dichotomy,
I don't understand it.
Except in football,
I don't understand nations,
While you said Germany.
None of that matters
While we're between these sheets
With all this chemistry.
The inside of both our brains
Can't be the only location,
Which one of us wants to blink first,
The candles crackle in the bathroom
As the moments of the sun
Between the clouds is just a burst.
In another life
These words would make sense beyond us,
You phone me
Because you don't want to get the bus,
I accept,
Because I want to be with you sooner.

Szolnok

Blinded inside the pacemaker
Which tries to beat
With the natural light
On this solstice,
We'll be alive to burn out the wax melts,
And candlesticks.
Winter and lockdowns can't last forever,
They will never be able to justify
The loss of wealth.
My mind floats off with the ether,
I don't ask for much,
Don't allow people to recreate history,
Didn't we learn anything
From Spanish flu
And the latter day bolsheviks.
It's a mystery.

Pihlaka

When asked beyond writing what do I study,
I only say Valeria,
Does that make me an anthropologist?
I get lost in my thoughts in the bath,
Words and sounds bombard my brain
It's all wrath,
Everyone mistakes my real profession
Am I an etymologist?
You know,
I could be terraforming an idea to words,
But I find myself unable to explain
How you're the premise to this show.
The roses in the lenses,
Nexus of this universe,
I'm just a nerd.

Kaubamaja

I'm transfixed
On how you're dancing in my shadow,
Moves like cinnamon,
Addictive like tobacco.
If anyone was able to resist you
That would be called discipline,
Did I intend to bring a New York flow,
Lost in the afterglow
Of words about both you and home.
I didn't follow a discursive synonym,
Waiting for a shipment
Pronto or expensive centromin.
Hazelnuts and white chocolate,
The steam produced could revive an orchid.
Thanos couldn't touch you
Even with the Infinity Gauntlet.

Sääse

I don't really know how to start life,
Then again who does?
The red lights we ran,
I counted five.
Then again
Still it could have been
More than what was counted as surplus.
Twas a vintage purchase,
Another time this wouldn't make sense,
But space and time
Don't always work in the present tense.
Our fused empathetic state,
The older I've got
The more I've learnt to understand,
Show compassion and wait.
All the while,
I couldn't imagine this life
If I wasn't to fight for you.

Laagri

I had a dream last night
That we went drifting
When leaving the city.
I'd never seen Saaremaa
And figured the BMW could manage it,
The wheel locks happen swiftly.
A circadian rhythm,
That floated in and out of our system.
I dropped the clutch,
And through the wheel spin
The traction almost glitched.
I remember you messing with the iPod,
Putting on that Incubus song
Wish You Were Here,
I knew it was smooth sailings
As soon as the chorus starts
And we breakaway in fifth gear.

Vabaduse Väljak

When what you wanted to do
Was stay in and share a bottle of wine,
You did yours
While I sat writing
What was both ours and mine.
The fairy lights in the vodka bottles
Creating ambience,
I daydream of you
Wearing that transparent dress,
The one containing sequins.
Our minds were drifting off
To different plains,
It all continues
Resembling a game of chess,
There's so many parallels
I lack the wisdom to explain.
Tomorrow we will walk the old town
Even with the fog,
When we go to leave
I know you'll be wearing
My white football socks.

Viimsi Keskus

Do you miss
When we'd stay up all night and talk,
Just talk about life.
You know who is my true desire?
You.
We've moved so far forward
From the start,
I now can't wait
Until I can get five dimensions deep
Into your heart,
Better yet your mind.
A quantum solstice,
That lasts more than a lifetime
To the equinox.
I was thinking,
And do you remember
Our first trip away?
We went to Paris,
And when waiting for the Metro at Goncourt,
I explained the wormhole
And how we were either side of it.
Do you think that version of us
Is still together?

Kotka

I asked you
Why you have never worn a football jersey
At a photoshoot,
You replied with
I've never had one
With the right number on the back.
In being told this I asked,
What is the right number?
Six.
I told you
I would make that right for next season.
You gave a smile and told me
That the photos I want to see
Will happen soon.
I can't help but smile.

Kullerkupu

How we have those moments of freedom,
Before sunrise and around midnight,
Those are just bliss.
That's just my insight.
Whenever someone tries to take our picture,
You always lean in for a kiss,
Like you can't let anyone
Share the moment of us together.
I'm not complaining,
Just observing.
The symmetry
Could be misconstrued as catatonic,
Your mother emphasised
How my eyes lit up at you;
What burns brighter Tsar Bomba
Or atomic?

Maisi

I stay up at night and wonder
If anyone would graffiti a mural to us
On the glass of a tram stop.
If only the city truly knew
What was going on with us,
Between the snowflakes
Of this eternal winter.
A drunk stumbles past me,
As I wait on a broken park bench
For you to finish work.
He neither noticed me,
Or could comprehend what we have.
The frozen lake
On the outskirts of the city,
We can ice skate on another day.
What colours do you think they'd use
Blues, whites and onyx?
And to answer that question
From this morning,
I rhyme everything so I don't forget you,
Call it mnemonics.

Karjamaa

Serenity,
that's waking up next to you.
I don't think I've told you that,
sometimes
I'm just too intoxicated to talk.
While if the next sixty years
weren't enough for us,
I'll stay with you
in the life after.
I guess I will have to wait
until you are awake
to pass on this information.
Some days I get an existential crisis,
am I overthinking this?

Randvere Tee

If I could include vinyl cracks
Into this documented life and idea,
I would.
The quality of the grooves
As I rotate around you,
Filling me up with ideas that I get lost in.
A fuse lit and ready to blow
From my old Records by Led Zeppelin,
Tribe, those Depeche Mode classics.
Sorry,
Sometimes I get inspired
And go off on tangents.
What should I cook us for dinner tonight?
Nebulas and black holes take place
Across the day and night sky,
But I'd rather be here,
Cooking for you.

Paberi

Don't tell me this isn't true,
And it's all a part
Of a waking life.
An idea that we all do.
Why not use the words we don't,
When you dance and it reminds me
Of that Soul II Soul artwork,
Just more mesmerising,
And with better footwork.
A video to play on repeat,
With that song I own on vinyl
And lyrics I misread.
If we had a time machine,
I'd take us back to the atoms colliding,
When all there was only
Dark and grey matter,
Planets and stars primitive,
Hurtling around in the madness
And finding their place in the scatter.

Kalmistu

This could have never been ephemeral,
So people don't get to see
What happens to us beyond
Their own colour spectrum.
The universe was impressed with us
In this instant,
Before returning to the organised chaos
As the collision of atoms all ebb and flow.
All those years ago
When you had blonde hair for months,
Reminding me of Gwen Stacy,
We should have gone to New York that time.
Could have caught a Lakers Nets game,
But we chose to see my sister.
Does time appear slower
As we're in continual winter.

Paekaare

I won't write about you for the pay check,
It's all blessings;
Words from this frozen tram stop
To the opus by Steinbeck.
This is eternally just dopamine in my mind,
Hiding inside the winter sunshine.
Do you remember a few years
Back when my nephew was four,
And he asked you
Who was your favourite Pokémon.
You told him you like Digimon,
He insists you're a Flareon.
You smile,
And ask when my niece is going to come over
And watch episodes of Friends,
I'm not too sure,
But the thoughts in my head
Completely transcend.

Haabersti Ring

I woke up this morning
And your wrist tattoo
Was resting on my face,
Double trouble
All worth it in time and space.
A lifetime as a goddess
Must be hard work,
You tell me it's only what I think.
Those messages when I'm on the grind date,
With both a smile and smirk,
I tell you a lucid memory
About a missing link.
It's irrelevant to think about a nebula
Across the cosmos or this state.
How they look
Like every aspect of life
Through a retina,
It could be pareidolia.
Anyway,
Honey roasted pecans,
No expiration date;
Not even the loss of twenty-one grams.

Kelmiküla

Nothing is too hard to find,
Dreams in public falling through our mind.
Do you think people understand
Just how we look at life,
With the future both ahead and at our side?
What else is there for us to do,
It's too late to step outside.
Shall we spin records,
Drink for the rest of the night,
Dance, I'll let you decide.
Next thing we'll know
Is it'll be an hour
Before we both start work,
On our next day off together
Shall we go to the cirque?
When the snow thaws out,
Do you want to ride through the city
On the bike?
Like what we did
Before all this
Caused changed.

Vikerkaare

If it wasn't for the left side
Of your hair being braided,
I wouldn't be able to get past the symmetry.
Mosaic that I stepped around
To admire in Tivoli,
Archaic words that fall in and out
Of being traded,
Sorry I should have said fashion.
I often think what would be different
If you hadn't gone to Thailand
When Covid happened,
It's like the world had us on entrapment.
A bolt in the blue,
Volts and the hertz manipulated
As you're learning
How to give us both new tattoos.

Rahumäe

While to the person who said
It should have been till death,
Clearly didn't ever spend time with you.
As clocks elapse
And nobody knows the truth
About what is the definition of words,
I wonder if you have any family members
That have asked when are we going to think
About a rebirth.
And when we're south of heaven,
It's where I'd rather be.
I couldn't think of the right word
To fill this section.
I guess the line needs to stop here.

Sillaotsa

If we became separated
By continental drift,
I couldn't envision myself with anyone else.
I would wait a year,
Or decades well into the fifth.
I still remember when you said
The thing that enraptured you in
Was how I write you to
The centre of this universe,
Now everything relaxes in white smoke
slurs.
I know when I get in tonight
You would be star-fishing,
And I'd have to slowly manoeuvre
My way into your skin.
Who am I kidding,
This is how we live now.
Ramen noodles tonight,
Try and tell me what you'd change
While we chow.

Kelmiküla

You'll never find me bereft
In this situation,
while if I act it,
It would only be for a second.
I'm grateful for everything.
And if I find myself
Gazing at another woman,
I know I'm the only person
Who has you,
And I'm a better man than that.
When I'm unsure if it's all serene,
That Talking Heads song
Plays like an ear worm,
Would I ever ask myself,
Well how did I get here?
This only needs to take place
Once in a lifetime.

Kadaka

A metronome that works to dictate to us,
I'd use it as an instrument,
Obtuse things exist.
One thing that you do
which I never say,
How much I enjoy the view
When I walk in on you wearing just my
shirt.
Levitating playing,
And your hips move in a way
That Bukowski would have described.
But he didn't get these luxuries at my age.
He always said
That life was a game of luck,
I guess we were winning
And the game of chess or baseball
Which we had invested in
Was paying dividends.
Would you agree?

Kolde Puiestee

I guess I write now with more passion
Than when my world
Was a labyrinth of flowers and churches,
Caught between the flora
And my esoteric observations.
A level of reliance blocked
Within these gerchas.
Birds flocked
It reminded me of herons.
Remember us in Central Park,
Those New York City bed sheets,
Memories that were tonight the spark.
My nephew interrupted us during dinner
To say how you look like Diana Prince,
I didn't know he had seen Wonder Woman.
Gal Gadot is magnificent,
Though I often see just a smile,
You still infatuate me on all levels,
As I roll off my vices.

Löwenruh

Did you ever think when we first started
All of this
That we'd have a room full of Lego
For when my nephew comes over?
I didn't know
It was going to go that way.
The vinyls and the books I expected.
That way we are each waiting
On the other to finish using the bath.
What am I talking about,
When you're done,
Get your coat and boots;
I want to take you out of the city,
So we can marvel
In the nebulas and starfields that span parsecs,
As you explain to me
How we're all the same atoms and matter.

Ussimäe Tee

I write your name,
In sharpie across the windows,
My spontaneous manner of upper and lower case.
I want more than life thinks we should have,
Blinded by you
I guess that makes you my hero.
An elevation,
Euphoric guitar solo,
When all I could hear
Was someone channelling their desire
For their woman.
I understand him.
Then there's lightyears
Between cessation breaths,
I listen to you
As you ask me to get petunias.
Who is anyone to define what happens
Between our sheets,
I won't rest
Until our city knows the name Valeria.

Keemia

Up at night
As we're eating Belgian chocolates in bed,
You look over
On the pages that I read.
Holding back
So you can see the pictures
That my friends paint,
I couldn't write like them,
My words aren't tamed.
This was a conversation in the midnight hours,
You wearing an old band T-shirt;
That was an early date of ours.
I wish I didn't giveaway my Prince T-shirt,
Now ceramic words all whisper.
Spasmodic ideas,
Even though my brain is flooded
With the memories
Of all those galaxies and stars,
Those ones last night
Away from the light pollution.

Laulupeo

Ethereal lights
And you complain your feet are cold,
These winter nights feel eternal,
Either side of this mortal being.
While those brief moments
That hold the summer together,
I spend every morsel
Of the fragments of time with you;
Before a change and it becomes
Heavy weather.
It makes zero sense,
Like when I try to speak Russian to you.
The astronomical glitches that happen,
The blue, black and white
In the magnolia sky,
Lost in pareidolia
Unable to explain why.

L. Koidula

I know I don't want to have this conversation,
This is our home,
And this used to be their land.
So was there,
Is this a 21st Century imperial movement?
What will happen?
Do you want to move?
I switched off the news,
Tonight this isn't for me.
Did I say too much?
I listen to everything,
The moments between our heartbeats,
How you say my name when you're mad with me.
Seriously, this is all going to shit;
I don't want to wake up mourning,
Words for old friends
Isn't what I should be writing.

Salme

About last night,
That's not relevant
To the conversation this morning.
You know I'm lost
Between those heavenly eyes
And the dawn light,
I'm just looking you over,
An art form
I've done ten thousand times before,
Either from afar or closer.
Tonight shall we go to the old town,
Find an unvisited bar?
Can't Stop is playing,
Mistaking the Tornado with a Fender Jaguar.
I don't understand the barman,
Can you order for me?
The waitress said she passed us on the street,
I've been feeling pensive and distant,
A permanent fix
Doesn't happen in an instant.

Kalarand

A week is a long time
In any aspect of anything,
The sun was out today,
I wait for you by the seafront.
That's rare for this month.
The rough waters
Of the Baltic,
Is today Wednesday?
The sounds of the sea could be euphoric,
You didn't recognise the song playing,
It sounds lost.
Your eye drifts away from life,
Trying not
To think about the world at large.
I guess that was both of us.
Conspiracy theorists
Start to fill up both of our news feeds,
I think I will delete Facebook for a while.
I know this world makes us heavy mental,
It was lacking colours
When we got down to the ethyl.

Pikaliiva

Magnetic lines
Feel their way out of ideas,
As I trace
The contours of your skin.
Midnight dress
On your white skin,
It's all reminding me of zebras.
We look past the light pollution
As astronomical glyphs
Become traced through the sky,
Nebulas beyond our eyeline,
Poet by The Family Stone
Words from Sly.
Every word located between my bookends,
Would last longer
Than the remnants
Of my solstice footprints.

Kadriorg

We looked up prices
For hotels in New York City,
And the gentrification
Since Livin' La Vida Loca was real.
Do you think they knew the ramifications
Of the purge
And what was meant to be filthy.
I was hoping for romance,
The words fall far too short
Of how they should have appeared.
I am never fully sure
Of a dictated sentence,
A falling of ideas
As they become transcendence.
Nothing really matters
When you take up more than places in my mind,
How long before we go
Further dimensions deep?
We're at the fifth,
Should we reach the ninth?

Reisisadama A-Terminal

On those rare clear days
I can read your mind,
The stillness of the Baltic glistens
Out of the window of the coffee shop.
Fragile like the cracks in my hands,
What expands in an instant
With how the universe combined.
The riptide has calmed
Even if it's only for a moment,
The past fades into the ether,
Sapphires and emeralds collage the sea.
I'm tongue tied on the gemstones
That occupy your eyes,
My heart softened,
The internet would make it a cybertrend.

Kumu

An under appreciated moment,
Ripped jeans
That failed in the document.
Desiccated collard green,
Whiteout sun hiding behind
The taste of almonds,
While you're constantly
The life chess queen.
Has anyone ever seen
The manipulation of an hourglass
Like how I control our time together.
The upstream river
Hidden by the dead of night,
Seashells often spell out our name,
Salt and vinegar
With you in the picture frame.
All I know,
The fluctuation of time
Isn't beyond the realms of cards
In poker or tarot.
I enjoy being trapped in this moment,
Unlike a chicken in its cage.

Kaasiku

You remember that drive that we took
To your hometown,
Coconut scented hands,
And your hair wasn't your own.
You said we were meeting your mother
For coffee,
She struggles with my accent.
I am sure it was my genesis
Within this edifice.
She talks
Either too fast or too slow for me,
But more importantly
I can't always decipher
Her proverbs and metaphors.
You just smile
As she says what she says.
All the while
The antiquated songs and elevator music
played
With me unaware
As to how I should react to it all.

Rocca Al Mare

The coffee froze like the Baltic,
Static in the airwaves
And a misunderstanding to the aortic.
A stranger surfing
Above the sea graves,
What kind of sociopath
Would willingly expose themselves
To frozen rogue waves.
Monochrome lipstick,
That was new for you,
How have I managed
A decade with you impolitic?
Dried out spider plants
Hang from the ceiling,
The curl collapses
And I die inside
That they're still breathing.
We need to book a new tattoo together,
What colour seems like lemon meringue?
Closed question.
Black resembling the evening or morning
When all it was was your eyeliner,
The day stays ice cold
Like a stenographer's typewriter.

Lepistiku

Were you with me
The first time you heard
Come Away With Me?
The candles all have their cessation
In a spasmodic fashion,
Remember our face when we discovered
The region of Bashan.
It still doesn't sound real,
Brandish and almost an accent mendivil.
Knee deep in the waterfall of words,
A third of the actions carry traction.
I wouldn't have a cut on my thumb
If the neighbours
Didn't feel the need for the volume
Of their television.
Time falls out of itself,
What do you think the truth
Was with the Antikythera Mechanism?

Kalevipoja

I've seen you so many nights when I sleep,
It's true
That you occupy the space there
Rent free.
I counted words and syllables
Before all this,
How did my brain know you were this enigma
I had to have in an expanding corner?
I won't ever know.
I guess it was something
Locked in the layers of my psyche,
What do I know today?
I guess it doesn't matter
That it's not cryptic
That you're my resurrection,
Periodically my table and chairs
Arranged with you at the centre,
Clearly you're my predilection.

Lubja

Nothing can ever see itself
From the heart
Of a different macrocosm,
A blank word like an esoteric thought
Deep in the spider-verse,
Rounded off to the nearest dozen.
Coffee grounds
And you're my Gwen Stacy.
I guess that I had gone crazy
Like Seal, maybe.
It's all hibernation,
I knew I was going to spend it with you,
No matter how brazen
That sounds.
The sun is being held up at the junket,
And I read that Claude Monet
Could see ultraviolet.
I'm jealous
That he could see a world
That I will never be able to see.
Then again,
He never got to muse over you.

Roheline

Started off in time before morning,
Dawn goes past
As if it were overflowing,
One of your eyelashes
Caught on my fingertip.
But it's alright,
Oh it's alright.
I wonder if I should go back
To being a baker,
But I'd miss out on moments like this.
You would still be
The most prized possession
In the delicatessen.
Almond croissant,
I couldn't write it
In my graffiti font.
Then our evenings wouldn't consist of us
Sleeping on the sofa,
If I went back as a baker
We wouldn't be able to observe
Distant supernovas.

Tihase

And the waitress pours the coffee
At the table next to us,
Her shoes match the same ones
As those you wore yesterday,
He must have been an architect
As the only word I understood
Was that of the word truss.
I found I couldn't explain it
Unless I drew a design,
I guess he'd know we were eavesdropping.
The smile given
Was because you knew
I was starting to grasp
The difficulty of the language,
The holes in your jeans
Which I could have fixed with a backstitch,
The waitress asked if we were alright,
I just said I was vegetarian
So no meat on either sandwich.

Toompark

Children make snow angels,
And I never got to do such things
During my puerility,
Spiderweb hanging from the tree
Is getting frostbite,
It'll be months
Before anyone touches the public tables.
Faint notes from a sound
That's not fully on my spectrum murmurs
Into my eardrum,
Vibrations falling through me like a
meteorite.
We stand together
And in the moment before we kiss,
You draw my attention to a couple
Who share a single track of footprints.
All because she isn't prepared
For the permafrost,
I guess he had so much more
Than what she originally thought.

Angerja

While this life with you
Is a lucid adventure,
White shoes worn on the far side
Of the city walls.
Cowgirls out on a hen night,
I recognise one from a past life,
A look and smile before they were forgotten
To the vodka laced nights
And bright lights of the city.
Twisted metaphors with drifted resource,
Back as I remember
It all started when we first spent December,
Dancing between bar stops,
Braille menus have desires
Laced into laptops.
I'll spend the time
To write a word that's unique,
And you borrow my T-shirt.
Nobody else silhouettes
The waking life dreams quite like you.

Rummu

I know that eventually my words
Won't be clutch,
It happens to the best,
That cliché line
I don't wish to waste my time on.
So the point that my hands and cataracts
Start to fail,
That was the result of life and work;
Not neglecting,
I will always promise you that.
I guess that's why I try to keep our world
With new shapes,
So the inevitable future
Keeps itself temporarily distracted.
I've stained your perfume on me
That even if you're to flatline before me,
The Alzheimer's that would have stricken me
Wouldn't be able to erase you.

Viru

Happy birthday,
What more can I add to our world?
Age has always been irrelevant
Since we've been together.
Did I ever think
That something taking place
In the middle of a compressor,
Would become an infinite amount of semesters.
You and me with this blood sandwich,
The fights we had with and for each other,
Have you counted
The number of butterfly stitches.
I think you know
This is something I'm willing to die for,
The Baltic is rough waters.
So many different things mashed together
As our life score.
The heart is more
Than a blood pumping vessel or vacuum.
Though just so we're on the same page,
If I had 100 pages to show what you mean to me,
I'd cover your eyes
And describe my world without you.

adam Shove is an Estonian English poet, who writes poems laden with cryptic metaphors and pop culture references; doused in vodka and thrift shop ideas. Inspired by Aesop Rock, Frank Ocean, J Dilla, secondhand clothes, models, tattoos and expensive cars.

RELEASED BY DARK THIRTY POETRY

ANTHOLOGY ONE
THIS ISN'T WHY WE'RE HERE
MORTAL BEINGS
POEMS THAT WERE WRITTEN ON TRAINS BUT
WEREN'T WRITTEN ABOUT TRAINS
CLOSING SHIFT DREAMS
DESIRE

Printed in Great Britain
by Amazon